T0148560

FROM
ZERO
TO
INFINITY

The Mathematics of Success

Edwin DePaula

WESTBOW®
PRESS
A DIVISION OF THOMAS NELSON
& ZONDERVAN

Edition published by
CreateSpace, an Amazon company - 2014
Charleston, South Carolina, USA

Cover and interior design
Brenda De Paula
info@zerotoinfinity.org
Cover and interior images
Shutterstock

Translation
Sarah E. Green

WestBow Press books may be ordered through booksellers or by contacting:

WestBow Press
A Division of Thomas Nelson & Zondervan
1663 Liberty Drive
Bloomington, IN 47403
www.westbowpress.com
1 (866) 928-1240

ISBN: 978-1-4908-7229-2 (sc)
ISBN: 978-1-4908-7230-8 (hc)
ISBN: 978-1-4908-7228-5 (e)

Library of Congress Control Number: 2015903643

Print information available on the last page.

WestBow Press rev. date: 03/09/2015

CONTENTS

DEDICATION

This book is dedicated to my beloved children, Christian and Christopher. Once they are old enough to read these pages, I hope that they will be able to use this guide to reach their goals and make their dreams come true. But most of all, I hope that this book, which comes from deep down in my heart, will help them to follow in the footsteps of our Lord Jesus Christ, because He will undoubtedly lead them to infinity, to eternity!

FOREWORD

FROM ZERO TO INFINITY is one of the most interesting personal motivational books I have ever read. This work's content, simple and yet profound, captivates the reader while surrounding us in practical lessons that motivate us to be successful in any journey we decide to begin.

One way or another, we all want to succeed in different areas of life, and we also want to achieve new goals and increase our potential. The world is full of people who are frustrated because they have failed to achieve their goals, but I want to tell those people that a book like this one is like finding an oasis in the middle of the desert.

With great ease, Edwin De Paula provides us with convenient tips, creatively using mathematical principles to take us on a journey to fight for our goals. He helps us dream, and learn to face the challenges we will certainly come across; in short, he helps us make sound life decisions. De Paula motivates us to aspire to the very best, regardless of the obstacles we may face, stressing that we all start at "zero" before finally reaching our objectives, our "infinity."

The author tells us that "zero" is a starting point, and that we shouldn't go back there once we've left. I enjoy the way he motivates us to assess and study ourselves, to write about our challenges and goals, while also providing us with the tools we need to overcome and achieve them. He also recommends that we find a mentor who will listen and guide us in life, because no one is an island; rather, we are all beings that depend on each other.

De Paula also reminds us that we should keep a positive attitude, and he gives us interesting guidelines for addressing failures in life and coming out victorious. He also encourages us to find our absolute value, which is not based on what we have, but on who we are as people. In this book, you will find the principles and experiences that shaped the author and how those principles can help us and be a source of inspiration for our lives.

Finally, FROM ZERO TO INFINITY shows us the ultimate goal which every human being must achieve in life to be happy, a goal that transcends our temporal existence on Earth and extends toward eternity. Therefore, dear reader, immerse yourself in this book regardless of your current situation; I guarantee that you will be greatly inspired!

Andrés Peralta, M.Div.
Youth Ministries Director
of the Greater New York Area

ACKNOWLEDGEMENTS

I thank God for giving me the opportunity to live and use this book as a way to share my experience with others. Thanks to my beloved wife, Brenda, for being my constant companion, and for her love and support.

I thank my parents, Francisco De Paula and Severina Adón, for providing me with the human values that I can now share in this publication, as well as my sisters, Carmen, Kenia, Nancy and Grisobel, for accompanying me on the first part of my life's journey.

I will always be thankful for many others who, directly or indirectly, merit a mention. Teresa, Jorge, Mario, José, Francisco, Dignora, Silvia, Helaine, Argenis, Oscar, Henry, Argentina, Griselda, Davis, Mariel, Jonathan, Esquivil, Aracelis, Ydelci, Rosanna, Caonabo, Claris, Moisés, J. Coxaj, J. Andrade, Raysa, Julio César, Kathy, Alessandro, and everyone who made life a bit easier for me, thank you all for helping me reach infinity.

Special thanks to Dr. Gerson P. Santos, Pastor Andrés J. Peralta, Pastor José Carpio, Nelly Harris, Esther Adames, Rud E.

Ledesma, Alerson Jaquez, and Dr. Ronald Rojas for their invaluable contributions to this project. I also thank U.S. diplomat Michael B. Doyle, wherever he is serving his country right now.

Infinite thanks to all of you readers, my most sincere thanks and love to you all!

FROM
ZERO
TO
INFINITY

∞

INTRODUCTION: ZERO

"I am Alpha and Omega, the beginning and the end."

Jesus

The book you have in your hands did not appear out of thin air. Rather, its origins lie in years of frustration, hopelessness, unknowns and unfulfilled desires; the lowest rung on the ladder to success: zero.

Writing involves sharing, which is why I invite you to look through the following pages and delve into my world. There, I hope to share a myriad of experiences with you, some real and others imaginative illustrations. FROM ZERO TO INFINITY will attempt to explain the relationship between nothingnesss and everythingness, employing the concept of infinity as a guide. It will try to distinguish between scarcity and abundance, between the human and the divine.

The following pages will provide you with some explanations, and as we move forward together in our journey, I will show you that the most important thing in life is to keep growing until we are able to achieve our full potential; some refer to this systematic advance as *progress*.

My main objective in sharing these lessons with you is to demonstrate that all human ideals and dreams have a starting point and an end point, also known as a *goal*. And all goals are equally valid within this model; you may aim to lose weight, or perhaps you aspire to be accepted to Harvard University. Either way, I hope that this guide will help you make your goals a reality.

I have always admired the struggles of those who have fought to reach their goals. That's why I will not stop at sharing my own personal experiences; I will also discuss other people's stories, people who, just like you and me, once lived under the pressure of intense frustration, extreme poverty and despair, or great agony. Many of them conveyed their values to us using key phrases. Today, we quote and repeat those adages which motivate us to keep moving forward.

Mathematics is the perfect tool for illustrating the application of abstract concepts to everyday life in a way that is practical and makes sense. And mathematics is said to be a perfect science. It doesn't matter if it was your favorite class in school, or if you're not a big fan of math. Regardless, I hope that by the end of our journey, you are able to see the other side of this science: **the mathematics of success**.

I once read that, "Books are the bees which carry the quickening pollen from one to another mind." I hope this book enriches your life and helps you to grow.

Zero symbolizes beginnings, so I congratulate you, because you've started a new chapter in your life and I encourage you to enjoy every day of it.

0

*"I will bless you with a future filled with hope—a
future of success, not of suffering."*
Jeremiah 29

MY STARTING POINT

Take a moment to write about your current situation in the lines
below. You can include any or all of the following topics: spirituality,
finance, relationships, health, education, and philanthropy.

_____

_____

_____

_____

_____

_____

_____

_____

_____

_____

_____

_____

_____

CHAPTER 1

∞

ONE. THE BEGINNING OF YOUR JOURNEY

"A journey of a thousand miles begins
with a single step."

Lao-Tzu

M any years ago, I heard the above-mentioned quote in a radio commercial advertising alcoholic beverages. What I couldn't figure out was if the publicist was referring the journey a person might take from a simple "social drink," only to end up another victim of alcoholism. Of course, the goal of the advertisement wasn't to emphasize the dark side of alcohol.

Those who created that advertising campaign failed to convince me to buy the drink they were promoting. However, I must admit that although the commercial was unsuccessful, over the years, that quote has stayed as fresh in my mind as the first time I heard it. Why? Because it challenges you to start something new.

Nowadays, young people and adults face a common problem: they never decide to take that first step. Putting off a crucial decision in life is almost the same as never making up your mind to do it. In today's society, psychologists frequently use the word *procrastinate*, which is defined as "deferring or postponing."

I recently heard a speech by the great American motivator Jack Canfield in which he challenged the hundreds of people in the auditorium to act. He took one of the best-selling books from his *Chicken Soup for the Soul* series and slipped a $100 bill inside as if it were a bookmark. He raised the book high in the air and challenged the audience: "Which one of you would like to have this book?" The auditorium was packed. Five people stood up or raised their hands, but only one set off toward her goal. She stepped up onto the platform and snatched the book out of the author's hands. Canfield clearly had a plan, and he wasted no time in telling his audience that their actions needed to be a means of getting what they wanted.

We could compare the decisions we make every day to the steering wheel of a car: they may not be able to change the speed at which we travel, but they will most definitely change the course of our journey.

Decisions always start in the mind. In some cases, they emerge when we realize that the life we've lived so far lacks meaning, or that we have yet to achieve our full potential. That may be what triggers us to finally decide that something has to change. Of course, a decision that is permanently stuck in your mind won't do you much good.

Years ago, when I was just a kid playing little league baseball in my hometown stadium, I was selected to play on a team that would travel to Canada. I was eleven years old at the time, and unlike kids nowadays, I still didn't know much about the Internet or television. My world was not much larger than a small town on a small

Caribbean island. Canada? To be honest, I was more impressed with the idea of traveling on a plane than traveling to another country, but all of that changed drastically once I landed in that new country. After spending just two weeks there, my outlook on life changed completely. Every day was another step on a journey that taught me things that I had never even dreamt of before. I found new surprises at every corner: the airplane, our accommodations on the university campus, the little birds that hopped around in the green grass. I was astounded by the clean streets, the public transportation system, and above all, the amount of food we were served at each meal.

Canada became a synonym for happiness. To be honest, when you're eleven years old, you don't think much about eternity, but looking back, that country was the closest thing to the Promised Land that I had experienced in my rather short life. Our team won five out of the six games we played. Every day was a constant adventure: shops, trips, waterfalls, and above all, delicious food. For me, that trip was fourteen days of constant happiness.

When I got back home, I made a very secret decision that I would one day live in a developed country. My friend, it is never too early to make a decision. From that point on, I started out on a journey that, fourteen years later, would allow me to achieve my long-awaited dream of living in a developed country.

DREAMS AND DECISIONS

There's an old saying that, despite its simplicity, expresses a profound truth: "Dreaming doesn't cost a thing." Dreams are an important motivating factor that inspire us to act. Besides our most basic human needs, which, in my opinion, are the strongest motivators, dreams lay the foundation for the majority of the decisions we make in life. Perhaps what I like most about dreams is that they inspire us to focus on what we desire.

If we think about focusing on what we aspire to be or do, we must also consider one fundamental principle: the *beginning* of a journey is inspired by the *final destination* of that trip. The moment we identify our most important aspirations is the moment we take our first step toward achieving what we want to pursue in life.

We will use the concept of zero throughout this book as a simple symbol of beginnings. Some believe that zero is an empty symbol, that it is valueless. However, zero is simply a point that indicates where our journey toward success begins; we start at zero, and continue forward until we achieve whatever it is that we've set out to do.

Imagine that your dream is to travel to California, and so you decide to begin your trip in New York City. In this metaphor, New York is your zero, whereas California is your infinity. Do you get it? All goals are inspired by the future, and are marked by a starting point that helps us assess our progress. If we follow this analogy a bit further, you could use a mile-marker along the way, such as Chicago, to assess how far you had come or how close you had gotten to infinity (California). Having said that, if you lived in Utah and wanted to visit California, although the distance between the two points is shorter, you would never get to your final destination until you decided to set out on your journey. Therefore, no matter where you are, you will always have to make the decision to start your journey toward any goal, and hopefully you are making your first decision right now!

DREAMS HAVE NO LIMITS

Dreams are free and unlimited, and the human mind is our Creator's most brilliant work of art. Human reasoning is like the interaction between a computer's software and its CPU. All human beings are endowed with the same hardware; in other words, we all have a brain. However, every person will decide how to program their computer, their mind. This usually involves incorporating values we have learned from our parents or mentors and modifying them to make them our own. The society that we live in undoubtedly plays an important role as well, but in reality, we are the ones who decide how to program our minds: for good, or for bad.

"If your mind is conditioned to come to a standstill when confronted with the limits imposed by our society, you will bring the power of your imagination to a standstill and deprive yourself of the privilege of dreaming."

If your mind is conditioned to come to a standstill when confronted with the limits imposed by our society, you will bring the power of your imagination to a standstill and deprive yourself of the privilege of dreaming. The human mind has been the starting place for stunning works of architecture, spaceships, televisions, telephones, the Internet, airplanes, the radio, and all of the modern conveniences we enjoy in life. All of that started in someone's mind.

That ability to reason, think, and dream, given to us by God, is what sets us apart from other beings.

The act of dreaming is intangible and unreal; we could also say that it has no limits, and therefore, is an infinite act. Your goals and dreams can be as big and ambitious as infinity, or as small and static as zero. As you start out on your journey through life, remember that every day is marked by a starting point, and inspired by an end point, and you can get as far as you want. Also, the time it takes you to complete a journey will depend on when you decide to take off from your starting point after making the decision to achieve your dreams. Go ahead, make the decision to leave zero behind today!

1

"One day, Joseph told his brothers what he had dreamed ..."

Genesis 37

MY DREAMS AND ASPIRATIONS IN LIFE

Take a moment to list your dreams in the lines below. Don't limit your imagination. Dream big!

_____

_____

_____

_____

_____

_____

_____

_____

_____

_____

_____

_____

CHAPTER 2

∞

STAY POSITIVE

"The lifestyle of good people
is like sunlight at dawn
that keeps getting brighter
until broad daylight."
Proverb 4

Nowadays, we have everything we need to lead happy lives. Before the first humans came into existence, God had already created everything that they could ever need. Throughout our life's journey, we must understand and accept this truth; if not, we will constantly be chasing an impossible goal, one that does not exist.

Anything that you might need in life, the Creator has already prepared the world to meet that need. Look around you and think about everything you have within your grasp instead of worrying about those things that you wish you had. What you have is your starting point, and what you desire represents your goal or end point. Remember, the end point will inspire and focus you, although it could also become an overwhelming source of torture if you concentrate too much on what you don't have, and you could risk moving into negative territory.

LESS THAN ZERO

Living on the positive side of life means valuing and appreciating our starting point, zero. In the world of real numbers, zero is not a valueless number. Just as there are an infinite amount of positive numbers, there are also an infinite amount of negative numbers. Let me clarify this concept a bit more. Imagine you have $2 and you need to purchase an item that costs exactly $2. After making your purchase, you run out of money; you are left with $0. Now, if you have $2 and the item costs $5, you might have to borrow $3; or you could pay $2, and finance the remaining $3. In either scenario, you would end up with a negative balance of $3. Following the same reasoning, you could save a million dollars, or have that same amount of debt. If we think about it linearly, whatever you don't have is to the left of zero, and what you have is to the right.

The world of abstract numbers reveals an important lesson: we must learn to live on the positive side of life.

"Living on the positive side of life means valuing and appreciating our starting point, zero."

The tools or resources we have will help us to achieve our goals and objectives, and our most precious tool is life itself, which is a divine gift. Other treasures in life include our parents, spouses, children and friends.

My friend, the fact that you are reading this book means you have one big advantage over many people who cannot do the same. For example, thousands of blind people study and, after much effort, are able to become successful professionals, while thousands and perhaps millions of seeing people are illiterate. Perhaps you have heard or read about all that Helen Keller was able to achieve as a young blind girl, or about Beethoven's struggle with deafness. They learned to maximize their resources instead of complaining about what they lacked.

The things we don't possess or don't have much of are not always a disadvantage. In the United States, obesity, especially childhood obesity, has become a national epidemic that affects hundreds of thousands of children and adolescents. This ailment can result in premature diabetes and heart disease, as well as emotional problems such as low self-esteem and trouble fitting in with peers. On the other hand, in less developed countries where children eat small portions of food due to their country's economic situation and a shortage of resources, we find lesser instances of this illness.

So, when you start your journey in search of success, remember to start off on the positive side. Whatever your goals may be— economic, entrepreneurial, personal or spiritual—remember that zero represents your starting point, and that from there, you must always move toward your goal, toward infinity.

SWIM AGAINST THE CURRENT

When I was 11 years old, after my inspiring visit to Canada, I decided that, one day, I would live in a developed country. The main options I was considering at the time were Canada, the United States, Spain, and Japan, in that order. Any decision we make in life is challenged by adverse circumstances, and I call that "swimming against the current."

And those challenges weren't long in coming. In fact, three of the four countries I was interested in presented one huge barrier: *the language.* Moreover, the process of immigrating to a new country is in and of itself quite challenging. Therefore, the most sensible decision I could have made at that time would have been to give up on my dream and accept reality.

I must confess that, for a long time, I pushed my dreams of traveling, studying, and living in a first world country aside. It's normal for us to avoid challenges. All rivers flow along the least resistant path. Predatory animals chase the weakest prey. Trees break at their weakest point, and humans adjust to easy and comfortable situations, avoiding those that require sacrifice or extra effort.

I wanted to be the exception to the rule, and so, throughout my life, I have had to learn to swim against the current. I discovered that any search is just as satisfying as the final discovery, and that the trophy a team receives at the end of the game is actually earned with each play. Yes, I have had to learn to block negative or skeptical thoughts that made me doubt my possibilities.

If I had relied on statistics, I certainly would have predicted that I would ultimately fail to reach my goals. Getting the proper visa to immigrate or even just to study in the United States is usually only possible for people who already have relatives in that country. My dream required abundant financial resources, something that I lacked.

"By faith, Abraham ... obeyed and went,
even though he did not know where he was going."
Hebrews 11

My friend, in order to stay on the path toward success, you must put your positive attitude into practice. Think about your goal as if it were already within reach; visualize it and enjoy it from a distance. Get familiar with what you want to achieve in life. Learn to listen to others, but always be sure to reach your own conclusions. Learn from others' mistakes and experiences, but write your own story. Don't hold back. The climb may be painful, but when you reach the top, you will feel satisfaction as you look back on the effort and sacrifice you've made to get there.

Now, I would not encourage you to stay at zero. In fact, most people get stuck at the starting point. Their New Year's resolutions hardly make it to February. So, what kind of attitude should you adopt?

Imagine that today is yesterday and tomorrow is today, as if you could forget about everything you've done and start all over again. Take a look at nature, which provides us with countless examples of cycles. The sun rises and sets; it rains, that rain evaporates, and then the sun shines again; the seasons change year after year, and all of these cycles have a purpose. Learn from your body's natural cycles, as well: you get thirsty and quench that thirst with a refreshing drink; you eat, exercise, and sleep, and the next day, you need to replenish your energy, and so you repeat the cycle again. Our goals are quite similar. The joy that comes from small achievements is a simple boost that gets us closer to our final goal. However, every small achievement can be cause for a big celebration. Start celebrating your achievements today, and prepare to start again tomorrow.

2

"I've commanded you to be strong and brave.
Don't ever be afraid or discouraged! ..."
Joshua 1

Yes, you can!

Make a list of the people who have achieved goals similar to the ones you intend to achieve. Make a note of how they did it. If your goals have never been achieved, write down why you want to be the first one to do it.

_____

_____

_____

_____

_____

_____

_____

_____

_____

_____

_____

_____

_____

CHAPTER 3

∞

RELATIVE AND ABSOLUTE VALUE

"My darling, you are lovely
in every way."
Song of Solomon 4

The ruler we use to measure ourselves is largely responsible for the attitude we adopt regarding the results we achieve. In his famous poem "Desiderata," American writer Max Ehrmann writes:

"If you compare yourself with others, you may become vain and bitter;
for always there will be greater and lesser persons than yourself."

People, especially young people, are always comparing themselves to their idols, whether they be sports athletes, movie stars, media celebrities or social network personalities. Young people are constantly encouraged to look like people who are admired by others solely because of their physical appearance. But today's youth are not the only ones affected by this negative tendency. What about soap operas and movies that encourage infidelity, or married couples who spend their days comparing themselves to seemingly happy and successful couples? Undoubtedly, we are all affected in some way by the social pressure of the standards our society imposes.

Advertisers begin by creating needs, and then present their products as the perfect solution, often taking advantage of people's lack of identity. It could be a drink, a pair of sneakers, or a car, but the common denominator is often one of the models mentioned above.

There is one piece of advice that could help us to solve problems such as a lack of identity, anorexia, bulimia, low self-esteem, and so many other emotional imbalances that plague our era. We must change the ruler or scale against which we measure ourselves. The ideal model is not a sports star with his muscular biceps and pectorals, nor is it the beautiful girl on the cover of a magazine, with defined curves, big bust, and flat abdomen. The ideal model is God. Yes, my dear friend, you were made in God's image, and you must therefore reflect His image. Accept and value yourself as you are, with all your virtues and attributes.

"So God created mankind in His own image, in the image of God
He created them; male and female He created them."
Genesis 1

We all certainly have habits that we can and must improve, but what ruler should we use to measure our progress toward a goal or purpose? The answer is: yourself. Do you want to be healthier? Do you need to lose weight? Would you like to make more money or get better grades? Would you like to find your life's companion? If so, take note of your current situation and use it as a starting point (zero), and then set your goals and ambitions as the end point, as your destination (infinity).

Decide *today* to do better in business, to improve your physical appearance, your studies, your relationships, and all aspects of your life. Decide *today* to get rid of any bad habits. You could even quit drinking soda, a first step to keep from gaining any more weight. If you attend school or college, spend fifteen more minutes on math or any other subject as a way of improving your grades. Spend more time with your spouse and children, and your home life will improve. The longer your list of actions, the more results you'll be able to achieve. Put in your best effort, fight with all your strength, dedicate yourself completely, and you'll see the results. Don't compare yourself to the person beside you because you are unique and special. The Creator made you different from everyone else so that you could have your own identity. You don't need to be like anyone. You were created in the image of a perfect being, so be your perfect self and reach your fullest potential. Dare to be happy and enjoy what you have right now. Take a moment to reflect on the following statements:

> "It is theft for me to take any fruit that I do not need."
> Mahatma Gandhi
> "Let no one ever come to you without leaving better and happier."
> Teresa of Calcutta

Nowadays, most people believe that the more things they possess, the happier they will be. For example, some fast food establishments sell you a cup of soda with unlimited refills. At buffet restaurants, you pay a reasonable price to eat as much as you want. When you rent a car, it most likely includes unlimited mileage.

"People are not valued by what they have, but for who they are.
Remember that you are an expression of the infinite,
the very image of the Creator."

You will also find, without looking very far, cell phone plans with unlimited minutes and data. If you understand where I'm going with this idea, it's a good time to reflect on the following questions: why would I want unlimited refills if my stomach has a limited size? How many cell phone minutes can I really use? The answers to these questions may be irrelevant, but we must bear one thing in mind: wealth only gives us relative happiness, and satisfaction is inversely proportional to need.

Allow me to explain this concept: imagine that you are running a marathon, and when you get to the final stretch, panting and thirsty, your friends give you three bottles of water. You drink the first one as if it were the first raindrop after a long drought. You drink the second one a bit slower as you chat with your friends about how difficult the race was. By the time you get to the third bottle, you might not even drink half of it. What happened? Your need for water lessened as you quenched your thirst. This explains why some people who have tremendous fortune, fame, cars, and romantic relationships get tired of it all, and in their insatiable quest for pleasure, they put all of their energy into acquiring meaningless material goods instead of focusing on what will truly make them happy.

ABSOLUTE VALUE

In mathematics, the absolute value of a real number is its numeric value without regard to its sign, which could be positive (+) or negative (-).

If we apply this definition to our lives, it becomes clear that our absolute value depends more on what we are than how others measure and label us. A few years ago, I read a few verses by famous poet Rubén Dario which do a very nice job of representing the concept of absolute value:

"A drop of mud
can fall on a diamond;
and thus, it can also
obscure its radiance.
But although the diamond
is full of mire,
the value that makes it good
will not be lost for even a moment,
and it will always be a diamond
even if it is stained by mud."

The number of digits in your bank account, the size of your hips, the length of your hair, or the color of your skin are an integral part of you as a person. But to equate the value of a person with their social position, their physique, or their profession is a very common error.

Humans have a few things in common in terms of their bodies: we all have a trunk, extremities, and the same physical makeup. On the other hand, although our ability to reason and make decisions sets us apart from other creatures, our personal identity and individual character make each of us a unique being.

"You are a special diamond in the Creator's collection of jewels."

You are a special diamond in the Creator's collection of jewels. You are brighter than the sun at the brightest hour of the day. Sure, others may not appreciate your true value because you hide it behind a thick layer of "mud": makeup, clothing, or contemporary fashion. Some pollute their minds and souls' brightness with vices such as alcohol or drugs which cloud their vision and contaminate their lives. He who fails to recognize his true value as an individual, his absolute value, may quite easily suffer from a lack of identity. And a person's value does not depend on external factors, nor does it rely on relative values such as academic titles, friendships, possessions, or social labels that society has forced us to accept.

One of my favorite stories has to do with an ancient administrator. It can be found in the book of Genesis, Chapter 37, in the Holy Scriptures. Joseph was a young boy when he discovered his true value as an individual. His brothers sold him as a slave, and because of his dedication and loyalty he was later put in charge of his master's possessions in a faraway country. Years later, he ended up in jail for a crime that he hadn't committed. Despite his situation, Joseph stayed loyal to his master, even from the prison where he was located. One day, after much preparation, the young immigrant was given the opportunity to occupy a post that many noblemen, important figures, engineers, and citizens had hoped that the pharaoh would grant to them. Even his new title could not hide the brightness of Joseph's devotion, excellence and dedication; ever since he was just a child, he had done a good job of administrating the possessions that his parents had trusted to him. I'm not just talking about his integrity in watching over his parents' flock, but the fact that Joseph knew how to recognize the true value of a person, which is more than the value determined by his surroundings.

Look at yourself in the mirror. What do you see? I'm not talking about your appearance. What do you see? Look deep into your own eyes. What do you see? I'm not talking about your skin color, nor your size. Look through the window to your soul, your eyes, and go even deeper. What do you see? The answer to this question is your absolute value, because your face is the mirror of your soul. Your true value is more than just physical: your skin color, size, and shape are just the packaging. You carry the essence of who you are within you, in your heart. That's why you must always look for internal beauty, which cannot be changed by external factors that would normally affect our physical appearance. On the other hand, as the years go by, your internal beauty will become stronger, and like a sweet fragrance that cannot be hidden, it will touch all of those around you.

And if you're not where you want to be yet, don't lose hope! What's important is that you have persevered to this point and that you will continue on your journey, which is part of a finite and ephemeral life toward an infinite and eternal one. The most important thing on the Earth isn't where we are, but where we are headed.

3

"One's life does not consist in the abundance
of his possessions."

Jesus

THINGS YOU WOULDN'T TRADE FOR MONEY

Make a list of the your attributes and characteristics that give you value. What abilities, talents, or gifts grant you absolute value? How could you use them to achieve your goals?

_____

_____

_____

_____

_____

_____

_____

_____

_____

_____

_____

_____

CHAPTER 4

∞

SUBTRACTION. REMOVE OBSTACLES

*"What can we say about all this? If God is on
our side, can anyone be against us?."*
St. Paul

L imits are a part of mathematics, just as they play an integral part in our finite existence. We encounter limits every day, and are obliged to obey them; for example, we see limits when driving on the highway or using our bank account. Limits, barriers, or regulations can help us to stay on the right track, although they may be misinterpreted by many people, especially by young people. That's why we must differentiate between limits and obstacles.

All of us will experience a number of obstacles throughout our journey. They are a part of life, day in and day out. I know commendable young people who were unable to go to college due to a lack of economic resources, or because of their migratory status, or because they did not feel the desire to earn a degree. If you drive by a safety rail on the highway, that is also a limit. Now, if you are driving and you come upon an intersection that has been blocked off because of an accident, that is an obstacle that will not allow you to keep going. Limits help us to stay focused on our goals; obstacles keep us from moving forward.

LIMITS

"All things are lawful for me, but all things are not expedient: all things are lawful for me, but all things edify not." St. Paul

I have to admit that limits are not always pleasant, but they are there for our own good. Practically every country limits the amount of alcohol its citizens can consume before driving, a restriction aimed at keeping them from putting their own or others' lives at risk. Authorities can also establish a speed limit for a certain stretch of a road. A worried father can always place limits on his adolescent children to indicate what time they must be home. These are all examples of limits. Along our journey toward success, it is important for us to learn how to use limits to our benefit.

Limits can be an ally. Failing to respect them can lead to disastrous consequences, ranging from losing your parents' trust to causing the death of another person. Now, these regulations or limits can also become your enemy if they are applied erroneously or with bad intentions. There is a big difference between a limit that seeks to protect and a limit that is designed to manipulate and abuse others.

Some limits are established by people who do not necessarily have our best interests in mind, but who want to impose their ideas by force or deception. The objective of these kinds of barriers is to enslave and restrict us, so they are somewhat finite.

Do you feel pressured or restricted by an adverse situation in your life? As you read this book, are you suffering the consequences of an error that has taken away your freedom? Do you feel that you are the victim of an oppressive relationship, full of limits and rules imposed by abuse of power? I want to tell you that there is a hope for you to have freedom.

"...then you will know the truth, and the truth will set you free."

There is one place where no one can enforce any limits, and that is your mind. Our minds have unlimited potential; they can reach up high toward God's throne, and deep down into the depths of our souls. But oftentimes, a large part of that potential is locked up. The mind is like a prisoner trapped behind strong iron bars of fear, frustration, prejudice, mediocrity, and a lack of perseverance.

"Our minds have unlimited potential; they can reach up high toward God's throne, and deep down into the depths of our souls."

The good news is that you are in control of your mind, and therefore, you can choose to be free from the barriers that you once forced on yourself, limits that may not allow you to reach your full potential. Free your mind right now and leave all hopelessness and bad thoughts behind. Allow your imagination to wander up to God's throne and to stay there until you discover the precious treasure you should search for in the depths of your soul.

OBSTACLES

> *"Get behind me, Satan! You are a stumbling block to me."*
> *Jesus addressing his disciple, St. Peter*

Once you decide to achieve a goal in life, your journey will never be free of one thing: *obstacles*. Life presents them to us with different names, sizes and origins, and they could even come from different directions. What's important is that we learn to recognize these obstacles so that we can overcome them. There's an old adage that says, "knowing is half the battle." So, the sooner you mentally prepare yourself to accept whatever obstacles life throws at you, the better equipped you'll be to confront them and overcome them.

The best way to identify an obstacle is to know exactly what your goal is. When you visualize your future and clearly know what your mission in life is, any detour from the path will be easy to identify and you'll be able to dodge any obstacles. This is one of the most powerful secrets that will help you be successful: Remove all stumbling blocks from your life!

Many years ago, when I decided to immigrate to the United States, I was able to perceive how this principle came into play in my life. My goals were clear and well-defined, but right away, I found myself confronting many obstacles.

In almost every major American city, there are people who are unable to find work in their professional field, so they end up working in jobs that are both economically and emotionally unsatisfying. Many lawyers work as bus drivers; civil engineers work as waiters; some architects clean offices. Every year, medical doctors, dentists, teachers, journalists, and a variety of professionals from different countries move to the United States, but are unable to work in their field. Many are forced to change their professions to work in other trades that, though honest and worthy, are far from what they spent years studying and training to do.

My experience was no exception. I came to the United States a few months after the fall of the Twin Towers in New York City. I encountered an endless list of obstacles. The United States was about to fight wars in several countries. The air of insecurity and fear in the streets was a barrier to finding a job. In addition, I was in a new place and was struggling to learn the language. As if that weren't enough, the culture and weather of this foreign country added to my unemployment issue.

MY FIRST JOB IN THE UNITED STATES

I sold my car and other possessions, which allowed me to round up a reasonable amount of money that I hoped would allow me to survive for about three months in my new country of residence. But converting a foreign currency into dollars isn't always advantageous, so I found myself needing a job long before I had originally planned.

Thanks to a childhood friend who is like a brother to me, I got a job at a luxurious Italian restaurant in downtown New York

City. The tips were the best part of the position, but unfortunately, my good fortune lasted just three months. Determined not to let such obstacles get me down, I got a job at another restaurant. But I was fired at the end of my first day. It was around midnight when I walked out into the light mist that evaporated before it even touched the pavement and smiled in disbelief. I looked up at the sky and exclaimed, "What am I going to do now?"

What do you do when you find an obstacle? Remove it! That's the simplest way of putting it. If life throws you a fastball, the best thing you can do is hit it! It doesn't matter what goal you're after: graduating from high school, saving money to get married, buying a car, finding a partner, or saving up for your dream vacation. Remember, the best things you can do is remove any obstacle that is separating you from your goal.

SUBTRACTION

"'Tis easier for some men to enrich themselves with a thousand virtues, than to correct one single defect." Jean de la Bruyère

Subtraction is one of the four basic arithmetic operations. It involves removing a certain quantity. The result of this operation is known as the difference. For example:

$$100 - 90 = 10$$
$$100 = \text{Minuend}$$
$$90 = \text{Subtrahend}$$
$$10 = \text{Difference}$$

The world of mathematics teaches us about subtraction, which, as its name suggests, has to do with removing something. If we apply the principle of subtraction to the obstacles that prevent us from achieving our goals, we will end up with something called difference. The following is a short mathematical outline that we can also apply to real life situations:

Minuend	Subtrahend	Difference
Student	Weekend parties	Pass all his classes
Young lady	Junk food	Ideal weight
Young man	Drugs	Freedom

Subtraction is not my favorite mathematical operation, because I prefer to think about increases, addition, and abundance. However, subtraction has become a fundamental part of my toolbox for success. Subtraction always has an element called difference.

The number one objective of subtraction is to find the difference. If you apply this principle to your life, you'll realize that people don't succeed because they want to be different, but because they are different. Many years ago, I heard someone say that most people work normal business hours from 9 am to 5 pm, but those who learn to swim against the current work from 5 am to 9 pm. The latter group will always reach their full potential and someday occupy management positions.

So, today, I challenge you to see the world from another angle, to use your imagination, to accept a paradigm shift, and to conquer the world. Mark that difference, wherever you are: at school, at work, in your home. Make sure that you are offering more than what is expected of you.

After being fired from that Mexican restaurant where I worked for only one day, I found myself in the same situation as millions of immigrants: just another professional wandering the streets of Manhattan, doomed to work in jobs reserved for those who do not speak the English language, who have no profession, or whose academic degrees have no validity in the United States. I stopped for a minute under the rain that sparkled under the street lamps and I made myself a promise: "I'm going to be different!"

4

"If you already know what to do and you don't do it, then you are worse off than before."
Confucius

THINGS THAT I NEED TO REMOVE

Make a list of friendships, habits or things that you need to remove from your life. Include everything that stands in the way of you making your dreams a reality.

_____

_____

_____

_____

_____

_____

_____

_____

_____

_____

_____

_____

_____

CHAPTER 5

∞

THE SIGN. CHANGE DIRECTIONS

"There are some things that people cannot do, but God can do anything."

Jesus

I n mathematics, the word *sign* refers to the positive or negative value of a digit or number. All non-zero integers are positive or negative, which is indicated by a sign. The same thing happens with real or rational numbers other than zero.

If we follow the mathematical model, we could say that the sign indicates where you are in relation to zero. In addition, this indicator can show if you change direction on the number scale. When you go from negative to positive numbers, the sign changes, so we could say that the sign is a signal of change. Likewise, throughout our journey to infinity, we will have to make changes to avoid obstacles, but without getting sidetracked from our desired goal (infinity).

*"Insanity is doing the same thing over and over again
and expecting different results." - Albert Einstein*

Deciding to change and break the vicious circle that separates us from our dreams is undoubtedly a wonderful thing, but unless we are ready to act, our dreams will never become reality. To be honest, none of the triumphant figures we admire reached any of their goals by chance.

Constant hard work is what allows champions to earn their title. You can't increase the size of your biceps after your first trip to the gym, nor will you manage to drop one size after just one aerobic workout.

Michael Fred Phelps was born on June 30, 1985 in Maryland, United States. Phelps started swimming at a young age, and by the time he reached the 2008 Beijing Olympics, he was already an internationally recognized figure. Michael Phelps won 22 medals over the course of his career, establishing new swimming records. What was the secret behind Michael Phelps' great success? His great work ethic. He saw the pool as his workplace, and he spent as much time swimming as any 9 to 5 executive. He was dedicated to putting in his very best effort in order to beat his own records. I call that an excellent work ethic.

Work is nothing more than a place where we put our inherited or acquired capabilities and talents to use in order to obtain results that will be beneficial for a cause. Companies hire employees to collaborate in the company's cause, and most of them agree to exchange their work for a wage. But that is precisely the worst motivation: working for money. Work should be the tool that paves our way to success. Think about this statement for a moment. Money is a simple tool used to transfer goods and services. So, if your only goal when working is to earn money, everything you do will be motivated by a transient and unstable instrument subject to inflation, loss and many other risks. Someone once said that, "money is a good servant, but a very bad master."

"The path to success has no shortcuts, but is a straight line paved with hard work and dedication."

The path to success has no shortcuts, but is a straight line paved with hard work and dedication. Work is your best friend. Would you dare to ask your best friend for clothes, shoes, food, shelter, or spending money? Maybe you would, but if you were to do so every month or every week, you would soon lose that person's friendship. However, as a faithful friend, your work gives you the opportunity to earn all the above-mentioned items without complaints. Work is a constant, obstacle-free source of resources, whether they be delivered every week, two weeks, or once a month.

MAGAZINE COVER CULTURE

In the modern world, we are taught to judge success as if it came on the cover of a magazine. These covers usually promote contemporary artists, models and athletes' sensuality, beauty and power. It's hard to appreciate the hours of rehearsal that a musician had to invest in order to record the album that made him famous, or the sacrifices a model had to make in order to reach her goals. In today's society, we only see the final result, bypassing the entire growth and development process. All successful people share a common denominator that drives them from their starting point toward their goal: *and that is work.*

After having experienced the disappointment of losing my first job in the United States, I made the decision to get a better one. That's when I realized that if I wanted a better job, I needed a better education. I recognized that if I wanted to increase my income, I had to maximize my potential. So I enrolled in college, which of course was very expensive for a foreigner. At that school, the only free program that I could take advantage of was a college-level English course that lasted about three months.

Before coming to the United States, I had worked in an information systems department. I had also worked for a few network and Internet services companies. Before leaving for New York, I was designated as the manager of a company that provided business services and high-speed Internet in my country. I hoped to find a job in my professional field, but that was very difficult, and I needed to survive and help my parents financially. During the following months, I had no income, and I remember crying out to God asking for an opportunity, and finally, He heard me. The pastor of the church I visited needed someone to clean the temple courtyard. Autumn brings many leaves, and I would be responsible for leave pick up at least twice a week. He offered me the job, and I happily accepted. Now that I had a job and had started attending college, I was on my way to success. At the end of those three months, the English course ended and the leaves stopped falling into the church courtyard, and once again, I found myself without a job and without studies.

"Not moving forward over time is the same as moving backward."

Someone suggested that I talk with my friends and acquaintances about my computer maintenance and repair services. That's how I found out just how inadvisable it is to be out of touch with the technology and information world. By 2002, Windows' operating system had been replaced by a new version, and to top it all off, I knew nothing about the new system.

Not moving forward over time is the same as moving backward. I was stuck because of my limited professional development. In the short six months since my arrival in the United States, everything I knew had become obsolete and trivial. My situation was a difficult one: I was in a foreign country, I didn't have a job, nor any way of getting one, and my skill set was outdated. I was far from my family and friends, and I realized that I needed to change something. I needed to find a job as a basic source of income so that I would be able to increase my earning potential; in other words, my main challenge was to earn more money.

5

"Actions should not be a reaction but a creation."

Mao Tse-Tung

ACTIONS I NEED TO TAKE

Make a list of the relationships, habits and things that you need to make a part of your life.

_____

_____

_____

_____

_____

_____

_____

_____

_____

_____

_____

_____

_____

_____

Chapter 6

∞

ADDITION. INCREASE YOUR POTENTIAL

"We know that God is always at work for the good of everyone who loves him. They are the ones God has chosen for his purpose."

St. Paul

S o far, in our journey to infinity, we have seen how important it is to identify your starting point (zero), and that we must stay focused on our goals (infinity). Our study of mathematics showed us that addition is the motivation that drives us from a starting point and gradually leads us to our desired goal. Addition is one of my favorite mathematical operations because it represents growth, prosperity and abundance. However, addition has one small problem: zero. Some call it the neutral element of addition. Why? Because no matter how many times you try to add zero to your repertoire, it will never represent growth.

Similarly, many people would love to increase and develop their potential, but they are stuck a state of inertia because they are unable to leave zero, or they simply get to a state of stagnation because what they are adding to their emotional, professional, or spiritual repertoire has no value whatsoever.

STEP BY STEP

"Grain by grain the hen fills her gizzard." Popular proverb

One of the many things I have learned since arriving in the United States is how to enjoy nature. For the first time in my life, the weather seasons made sense to me. Getting to know the four seasons of the year and living the emotions and expectations associated with each one is a wonderful experience. Each season brings its own joys and challenges.

SPRING
Spring represents joy; birds begin to chirp, flowers sprout, and trees become green again. People leave their heavy coats behind and feel the relief of warmth after months of harsh cold weather.

SUMMER
In some places, summer means intense and unbearable heat, but it is also a time for enjoying beaches, pools, and resorts.

AUTUMN
Autumn brings relief from hot temperatures and a pleasant atmosphere for enjoying parks, spectacular sunsets, and the changing colors of the trees. It provokes these changes in the trees so that they can survive a harsh winter.

WINTER

In the most northern regions, winter represents cold weather and snow, but it also brings warm fireplaces and winter games, as well as the indescribable Christmas atmosphere.

Part of my professional experience could be represented by the changing seasons over the course of a year.

FIRST SEASON (WINTER)

During my first winter, I learned that you can earn money during any season. Although there were no more leaves to pick up, I was able to continue working. I started clearing the snow off of the church staircases and parking lot. In that way, I was able to maintain my source of income for several months.

SECOND SEASON (SPRING)

When spring arrived, my life entered a new chapter. I thanked God and my church minister deeply for giving me work during the winter months, and now, I was ready to venture out and start moving up the professional ladder. I was presented with the opportunity of working as a cashier at a supermarket. I put in a great deal of hard work there almost all spring long.

THIRD SEASON (AUTUMN)

By the time autumn arrived, I had gotten a commercial license to drive school buses. So, I thanked the supermarket manager for the opportunity and I set out on my new adventure.

FOURTH SEASON (SUMMER)

As my earning potential grew, I also began to feel more confident and determined. So, a few months after the harsh winter had ended, I decided it was time to get out and conquer the world of employment in New York. For years, I had worked toward mastering the science of automated information (network engineer). God gave me the privilege of working for an international money transfer and currency exchange company. The salary for my fourth job in the United States had quadrupled my very first salary in this country and my new professional title was technical support.

Many people complain about their jobs, but mainly, they complain about their results. How was I going to increase the fruits of my labor and improve my income? This is where the power of addition comes into play. The answer is: increase your potential. In order to do that, you need to maximize your professional capabilities and knowledge to the fullest as you strive to reach the position you desire.

STAGNATION ILLUSTRATED

Many years ago, when we were still kids, my sisters and I loved it when our mother would prepare a special breakfast drink for us. It was a mixture of malt and sweetened condensed milk. Many of the most heated arguments during our childhood had to do with who would get the empty can of sweetened condensed milk. We loved opening the can and draining it until the last drop of milk came out. That day, after a heated discussion, my sister Kenia came out winning. I wasn't very happy with the situation, and upon accepting my defeat, I burst into tears.

My mother had the brilliant idea of ending the problem once and for all; she would simply throw the empty can away. My sister was quite clever and knew that she wouldn't have much time to open up that can of sweetened condensed milk, so she quickly stuck her tongue in a tiny hole in the can. She closed her eyes, giving off an air of emotional ecstasy as she enjoyed the last drops in the empty can. Suddenly, Kenia's eyes grew much larger than usual; it turns out that her tongue got stuck in the hole. After several minutes, many tears and much anguish, my sister was freed from her predicament, from her stagnation.

WHAT IS STAGNATION?

It is defined as "a failure to develop, progress, or advance." After finding the job I longed for in the field of information technology in the heart of New York, I thought my growth would continue on at a steady pace. However, I realized that such good fortune wasn't going to last. My income barely met my expenses, and my desire to go back to school and pursue further professional development was put on hold because of the high cost of education for foreign students. As if that weren't enough, I felt like I was working against the clock. It was clear that my professional life was suffering from *stagnation*.

DIVINE PROVISION

After 11 months, the company I was working for relocated, and when they moved, I lost my technical support position. Once again, I was back at zero.

As the days went by, I felt sure that I would get a job in my field, in information technology. But over time, my hope turned into distress, and my distress turned into despair. I spent an entire frigid day walking through the streets and dropping my résumé off at every business and computer repair shop I found.

Do you remember the minister I told you about earlier, the one that became my first employer? Once again, he proved to be my guardian angel. When he found out that I was unemployed, he decided to recommend me to a bookstore that he had worked at years ago upon arriving in New York. The only available job was a customer service position. I went in for an interview, and they offered me the job that very same day. Although my income would be practically half of what I had earned at my previous information technology technician job, in the end, that bookstore was the school that prepared me to work in the United States.

THE KEY TO INCREASING

The most important thing you must do to increase your income is to genuinely and vehemently want it. And although that is the most important part, it's not the only piece of the puzzle. Beyond having a deep and intense desire, you also need a plan of action to accomplish your objective. In my case, I carried my desire in my heart, but I had no idea how to do it.

My first instinct was to start looking for another job, so my plan went like this:

1. Update my résumé.
2. Create accounts for several employment websites.

3. Talk to my friends and family to let them know about my job search.

4. Frequently check the employment section of the classified ads in newspapers and magazines.

So, I had a desire and a plan. The only thing I was missing was more money in my bank account, so I sat and waited for my plans to come to fruition.

I'd like to tell you that I was able to increase my salary by some significant amount after waiting for just a short while. But that didn't happen because my first plan was a total failure. Six months later, I was still working at that bookstore, earning the same salary. What had happened? Had my formula failed? No. I still believe that a desire and a plan of action will get you where you want to be. My desire was obviously still there, so if something in my equation had failed, it must have been my plan.

I sat down and revised my plan, and I immediately found the problem. In all honesty, my plan was missing the most important component: education. Since we are living in the information era, the level of education that professionals need in order to compete on the job market is constantly increasing. So, I took another look at my plan and realized that I would need to become more educated than my competitors in order to get a job in my field. My plan changed, and it looked something like this:

1. Update my academic knowledge.
2. Update my résumé.
3. Create accounts for several employment websites.

4. Talk to my friends and family to let them know about my job search.

5. Check the employment section of the classified ads in newspapers and magazines.

Now that I was equipped with an intense desire and an updated plan, I was ready to increase my income. "Get ready world –I said to myself– I'm here to conquer you."

6

"Folks are usually about as happy
as they make their minds up to be."
Abraham Lincoln

SET OUT TO DEVELOP YOUR POTENTIAL

Make a list of the areas in your life that you want to improve. Don't worry about how you're going to do it yet. Just write down what you want to accomplish.

_____

_____

_____

_____

_____

_____

_____

_____

_____

_____

_____

_____

_____

CHAPTER 7

∞

DIVISION. DIVIDE AND CONQUER

"Start by doing what's necessary; then do what's possible;
and suddenly you are doing the impossible."
St. Francis of Assisi

The truth is, although a written plan may seem beautiful and even inspiring, in reality many young people and adults fail when attempting to put their plan into practice. Architects frequently have to change their plans and designs when the engineers inform them that their proposal isn't structurally sound. On more than one occasion, a web designer has had to change his original plan due to errors in the programming code. The point I want to illustrate is that even if you have an intense desire and the right plan, that might not be enough.

The following saying is very well known: "Easier said than done." And in my case, I had to learn that the stretch between saying and doing comes in different shapes and sizes.

GOALS

The Greeks used the word "μετά," which today would be the equivalent of the word "goal," and whose main meaning goes beyond the present; in other words, it implied something in the future. Likewise, the Romans used a similar word that may have had the same meaning. That root word is the origin of words like "meter," which is used for measurements. If we combine both concepts, we could say that goals are a practical way of measuring an event that we expect to happen in the future. In other words, a goal has to do with both the final destination or objective (measured in time) and the path that we must traverse to reach that objective.

There is one mathematical operation which illustrates how time and goals are related. I'm talking about division. Division is defined as follows: division is a "decomposition" which consists in finding out how many times a number (divisor) goes into another number (dividend). The result of division is called the quotient.

Division usually has a negative connotation because it always suggests the separation of a unit into several others. Of course, in certain aspects of life, one would not wish to have any such separation, like in a marriage. However, division has a very positive aspect, and it is quite applicable to daily life. A popular proverb says: "grain by grain the hen fills her gizzard." The main thing we learn from division is that you can complete a big task if you divide it into small actions.

DIVIDE AND CONQUER

Have you ever heard someone say: divide and conquer? I assure you that there is much truth in that saying. As we saw before, there are two main factors in division, the dividend and the divisor. Similarly, we could say that goals have two main parameters: the *objective* and *time*. These two parameters must go hand-in-hand if you want your goals to be effective, which is why goals should be measured with respect to time. In turn, goals can be divided into three categories: short, medium and long-term.

SHORT-TERM GOALS

A short-term goal is one that we aim to achieve within 90 to 180 days from the moment when we establish that goal. Short-term goals should be part of a long-term goal. They are simply an effective way of quantifying our achievements. For example, if your long-term goal is to become a professional guitarist, a short-term goal would be to buy a guitar. Having the guitar doesn't make you a professional guitarist, but if you spend time and effort with that guitar, you could eventually become a professional guitarist (thus reaching your long-term goal).

MEDIUM-TERM GOALS

A medium-term goal is one that will serve as a point of reference as we strive to achieve our final goal. The purpose of this type of goal is to remind you are more than half-way to your final goal, and to motivate you to achieve what you have set out to do. An example of a medium-term goal is to graduate from high school. You know that you must achieve this goal before you can be accepted at a university.

I remember the day I graduated from high school in the summer of 1994. Given my economic situation, I was unable to walk with my friends at graduation, but I did have the privilege of being a spectator at the event. Graduating from high school was always my intermediate goal. I dreamed of one day becoming a professional with a college degree, which made it easier for me to accept not being able to participate in my high school graduation. I never imagined that years would go by before I would be able to reach my final goal.

LONG-TERM GOALS

A long-term goal can be extended for several years and sometimes for a lifetime. As its name suggests, it is a goal that's further away. I reached my goal of getting married and having a family by the age of 28. Walking in my college graduation was something I accomplished 14 years after my high school graduation.

In short, goals demand focus, effort and direction. It doesn't matter if they are short, medium or long-term; your goals should be part of a strategy that will take you from zero to infinity.

So decide today which goals you will achieve tomorrow!

7

"My friends, I don't feel that I have already arrived. But I
forget what is behind, and I struggle for what is ahead
St. Paul

TURNING YOUR DREAMS INTO GOALS

Read the list of dreams in activity number 1 at the end of Chapter 1. Select your biggest dream and write about how you will turn it into a goal. Include a date that you would like to achieve your dreams by. Include even the smallest details and you can use an additional page if necessary.

_____

_____

_____

_____

_____

_____

_____

_____

_____

_____

_____

_____

CHAPTER 8

∞

MULTIPLY. GOD'S FIRST COMMAND

Then God blessed them and said: be fruitful and multiply;
fill the Earth."
Jehovah

Multiplication is a mathematical operation that can make a number grow as many times as the factor indicates. It is like a special kind of addition in which a number indicates how much to add and the other indicates how many times to add that amount. But beyond a mathematical operation, multiplication is a divine command. Yes, you read it right. That was the first command given to humans, to our first parents, Adam and Eve. How can we apply the principles of multiplication to achieve our goals?

We have to understand the laws that govern multiplication. Learning about such laws is vital if we want to effectively and efficiently move toward infinity. In the mathematics of success, we must avoid multiplying:

1. By negative numbers
2. By zero (0)

3. By one (1)
4. By a fraction

LAW OF MULTIPLICATION NO. 1
Never multiply by negative numbers

Multiplication is like a spring that can move you with incredible force toward a defined goal, but which needs direction. If you jump in the wrong direction, you could even end up much further away from your goals. This is precisely what happens when you multiply by a negative number. For example:

$$5 \times 4 = 20; \text{ whereas } 5 \times (-4) = -20$$

Did you notice the end result? One of them gets you closer to your goal, while the other can move you away at the same rate.

So is life, especially when it comes to associating with others. Build relationships with people who will help you get closer to your goals. Interact with people who can help you move forward and not backward. Stay away from those who are an impediment, like a girlfriend or boyfriend who wants to have intimate relations before marriage. You may originally see that person as something positive, a partner who wants to move forward with you toward your goal. Be careful! The truth is that all this could actually be a NEGATIVE sign: an unwanted pregnancy or a sexually transmitted disease. This kind of relationship, along with many other possible scenarios, could move you further away from your goals at the same rate as a relationship with a positive person (someone who values you for what you are and not for what he or she can get from you at a certain point in time) would move you closer.

So, start right now and make an inventory of everything around you, whether they be people or things, and be resolute in your decision to remove everything that you consider negative from your life. The law of multiplication is simple and clear. If something has a negative sign, it will not help you to move forward; rather, it will make you move backward.

LAW OF MULTIPLICATION NO. 2
Never multiply by zero (0)

"Never multiply by zero." This is an interesting law. The real objective of multiplication is to add in a systematic and consistent manner. However, when you multiply a number by zero, it is like losing everything that you've gained. Multiplying by zero is like a runner who sets off in a race before the judge says "Go!" and thus has to return to the starting line. Or like the case of a man who finds $100 on the sidewalk and decides to spend it all on lottery tickets to keep trying his luck and thus multiply his fortune, only to discover that he has lost everything. In both cases, it is the same as going back to the starting point: to zero.

Zero is an important point of reference in our journey to infinity. However, it is not the place that we wish to return to once we have left it behind. Try not to make unfounded, hasty decisions. For decisions like getting married or choosing a university major, you should pray to God and talk to your parents. Just one day, just one decision, is enough to send you back to zero. It doesn't matter if your infinity is getting out of debt or saving up enough money for a down payment on a car before going to college. Always pay attention to the second law of multiplication: "never multiply by zero." Lose that ALL or NOTHING mentality when taking risks. Constant progress and controlled risk is better than shortcuts. Remember that the race to infinity is about *endurance*, not speed.

LAW OF MULTIPLICATION NO. 3
Never multiply by one (1)

They say, "no one is wise in their own eyes." We will not be able to move forward in life if we only see things through our own eyes. Paying attention to others' advice, especially that which comes from individuals who are older than you or from people who genuinely care about you, is one virtue that you must develop if you want to be successful.

No person "is an island"; rather, we are all part of a continent. If you take a look at humans, even just from a biological point of view, you'll see that we would not be able to survive if we didn't function as a society.

Great care and much concern is required to raise a baby until she can fend for herself. Wisdom is passed on from generation to generation through questions and contributions made by those who lived before us. Today, we can enjoy huge cruise ships, airplanes, telephones, the Internet, satellites, cars, and smart phones thanks to the contributions that some men and women made to the field of science in the past. Likewise, you will need the people around you who have already traveled the roads that you will one day travel to give you their opinion and to guide you.

Mathematics abides by the following rule: "Any number multiplied by one (1) will result in the same amount." It doesn't matter if you're working with positive or negative factors; whenever you multiply a number by one, the result will be the same amount. This law is also called the "neutral element" of multiplication. Even if our ideas seem completely brilliant, if they do not pass through the filter of criticism or receive advice from an outside party, we will be unable to move forward. The third rule of multiplication in the mathematics of success explains that you cannot move forward if only you trust your own opinion, or the personal whims of your heart. The Bible says:

"The heart is deceitful above all things, and desperately wicked; who can know it?"
Jeremiah 17

If you want to be a doctor, try to volunteer at a hospital. If you want to be a congressional representative, start by understanding your country's laws. Seek the advice of those who have been around longer than you and thus have had more experience. Before making certain important decisions, make sure to talk to your parents, older siblings, pastor or spiritual leader. Always find a reliable point of reference. Remember: "in the multitude of counselors there is wisdom." Do not rely solely on your own opinion. Be wise and listen to the recommendations of those who are more experienced than you.

LAW OF MULTIPLICATION NO. 4
Never multiply by a fraction

When you multiply by a fraction, it has the same effect as when you divide, which will be contrary to what you want to achieve. That is, instead of moving forward, we go backward; instead of winning, we lose; instead of increasing, we decrease. For example:

$$20 \times 2 = 40; \text{ whereas } 20 \times \tfrac{1}{2} = 10$$

In the second part of the example, it would seem that the result is the opposite of the one you want. If you look carefully, you'll see that the sign is the same. The initial amount is the same, but the damaging factor is the fraction.

A fraction indicates that something is damaged or broken. The fourth rule of mathematics advises us that we should not associate with "broken" people so that we can continue advancing toward our goals (infinity).

Remember, never try to move forward (multiply) alongside someone who is spiritually or morally "broken" (their heart, or their principles and values). Surround yourself with upstanding people that will help you move forward instead of backward.

Study the laws of multiplication and you will reach your goal quickly and surely. Identify negative factors, avoid zeros, do not rely on your own opinion, and never associate yourself with people who are "broken" or suffering from moral or spiritual bankruptcy. Now that you have these laws in your hands, get up and go conquer infinity. Remember: multiplying was the first divine command.

8

"I run toward the goal, so that I can win the prize ..."
Philippians 4

CHOOSE A MENTOR

Choose a person you admire; it can be your father or mother, a close family member, a teacher, a pastor or a spiritual leader. Share your dreams with them. Listen to their advice. Write what you learned in the following lines.

_____

_____

_____

_____

_____

_____

_____

_____

_____

_____

_____

_____

CHAPTER 9

∞

RADICAL. CHANGE YOUR ATTITUDE

"for as he thinketh in his heart, so is he."
Proverbs 23

Working in a bookstore in downtown Manhattan was a wonderful experience for me. I learned how to interact with clients using the English language. I had the opportunity to read good books, and above all, I felt that more than working at a job, I spent my days in my school library, talking to my friends about my favorite books and recommending healthy food to our customers.

But although I felt thankful for that job, which had come as an answer to my prayers in one of the most difficult moments of my life, I soon began to feel that if I didn't change directions, my dreams would stop there. No! My plan was to achieve my goals, to reach infinity. I wasn't going to be able to reach my goal (infinity) of being a successful systems engineer in a developed country if I continued sorting boxes of books in the basement of an old Manhattan building.

I evaluated my situation and found that I was on a road that would take me precisely where, as a professional immigrant, I did not want to go. I didn't want to be like the Hindu physician who worked as a taxi driver in Brooklyn, or the Ecuadorian engineer who had reluctantly accepted life as a cashier in a supermarket in Queens. Just the thought of it terrified me, and with a greater sense of determination, I decided to make a change, a radical change.

RADICAL

Radical (from the Latin *radix* "root" or "base," something that effects the essence or the fundamentals; the deepest part). In mathematics, a radical is a very complex operation, but nowadays, thanks to computers and portable calculators, we can do it with the press of a key. I choose to highlight this complex mathematical operation because of its etymology, which comes from the Latin word for "root." When we think about this term, we are most likely reminded of plants. Trees and plants' roots are what help them stay firmly standing when winds and hurricanes blow.

I grew up on a Caribbean island, and my parents tell me that when I was just a baby, I survived one of the most devastating hurricanes to strike the region; I'm talking about Hurricane David. For many years, I wondered what it would be like to live through the effects of a hurricane: winds, rains, roofless houses, rivers overflowing, and of course, the loss of human lives. Then, in 1998, Hurricane George hit the island and, as an adult, I was able to witness the devastating effects of a hurricane firsthand. I was also able to contextualize all the stories that my grandmother and my parents had told me.

That hurricane resulted in immense material and human losses. But there was one thing that really got my attention: even though many trees fell, many others stayed standing. What made some of them fall, whereas other were able to stay upright? Their roots.

Their leafless branches painted a pitiful and despairing scene. What was supposed to be a tropical paradise now looked like a hospital or a cemetery of trees mixed with electrical cables. But in the midst of all the chaos, I learned that not all trees fall when the storm arrives. Many stayed standing thanks to the strength of their roots.

Your roots, in the mathematics of the success, are the support that will keep you firmly planted in the midst of problems and adverse circumstances. Every building needs a solid foundation that it can withstand the weight of the construction above, as well as the force of winds or seismic movements. The depth of the root and the type of terrain where the tree is to grow, or where the building is to be built, are important factors to take into account before planting or building. Likewise, in the journey toward our goals (infinity), every step that we take must be solid and firm, and should lead us to stable ground. After considering this concept and analyzing my options, I decided to do what I most needed to do to get closer to my goal.

BACK TO SCHOOL

Since I was unable to afford college, I decided to start at a vocational school where I could get the most current certification in the field of computer science. The program was expensive for my limited resources, so going into debt was my only option. There were many challenges. I had to pass fourteen rigorous exams over one year so that I would be able to compete for a place in my profession's job market. Even more, I had to work and comply with my regular 40-hour week schedule.

"To be a true champion, you must beat a worthy rival. If you are the favorite in the fight, there will be neither high expectations nor excitement when you win."

Dear reader, you have accompanied me on this journey to infinity, and I want to remind you that the most important things in life require sacrifices. We enjoy the reward much more when we have to fight for it. To be a true champion, you must beat a worthy rival. If you are the favorite in the fight, there will be neither high expectations nor excitement when you win. But if you're not the favorite in the fight of life, if the statistics show that you are destined to fail, then this is when you must prove to yourself and to the world that you are different and that the predictions do not apply in your case.

It doesn't matter if you're the child of divorced parents; you can have a stable, long-lasting and happy home. Even if you have a close relative who is in jail, nothing will prevent you from becoming a lawyer, a police officer, or simply a model citizen. If the statistics say that you will get pregnant and leave school before you turn seventeen, you can be the exception and wait until you graduate to form a home and raise your children. Even if a family member of yours died relatively young from alcohol abuse, you can live a sober life free of vices. Remember that David was not the favorite in the battle, but he turned out to be the champion when he beat Goliath (1 Samuel 17).

I was facing some big challenges back then. I worked from 9 to 5 in the afternoon, and then attended vocational school from 6 to 10 pm. Days turned into weeks and the weeks into months. Finally, after three months in that cycle, I was ready to take the first of fourteen tests I needed to get certified.

YOUR ATTITUDE IN THE FACE OF FAILURE

The day of the exam arrived. The woman in charge of the computer lab said, "Good luck," and left the classroom so I could concentrate on the task at hand.

The exam was very detailed and most of the questions had to do with real life scenarios. It was all too much for me, and I was defeated in the first of many battles. The result was disastrous and I failed the exam. Tears sprang from my eyes when I saw the grade I had gotten on the test. At that moment, I realized that I was living in a hurricane more powerful than David and George, which was called "the hurricane of failure."

Failure is the opposite of success. Failure has made millions of people abandon their journey from zero to infinity. Many people get stuck at zero due to their fear of failing at some point along their way to infinity. From zero to infinity, there are many failures. Countless young people and adults grow up with an immense fear of failure. Fear is a type of shelter that the Creator has put over our heads to sharpen our survival instinct. The emotion that we identify as fear is a necessary part of life, but when it grows and gets out of control, failure begins to feed on that fear, making us self-destructive.

So, failure feeds on our fears. I know young immigrants who can speak English, but since they are afraid that people will make fun of their accent, they don't practice it, and thus, they are never able to perfect it. I know students that are knowledgeable about a particular subject, but since they have a fear of public speaking, they fail the class or get bad grades. Therefore, I challenge you today to overcome your fears and stop feeding the negative thoughts that encourage you to feel like you've failed in life.

"People are not remembered by how few times they fail,
but by how often they succeed."
Thomas Alva Edison

However, failure has one weakness. If you manage to figure out what it is, you can beat it by using a peculiar resource: it's called *perseverance*. You will never feel like a failure if you keep making an effort. For example, on average, it takes a student four years to earn a college degree, but if you are a part-time student, it may take you twice as long to complete your studies. So, even if you are going into your seventh year in the engineering department, you have not failed to reach your goal, as long as you persevere and continue studying. Failure will not be a defeat until you accept it as such. As long as you are fighting to get ahead and overcome your fears and weaknesses, you have not failed. Each step you take from zero to infinity should remind you that you have not failed, but that you are still moving forward. A bump in the road can make you stumble and fall, but if you manage not to fall, you can use that momentum to quicken your pace as you continue to move forward.

"A bump in the road can make you stumble and fall, but if you manage not to fall, you can use that momentum to quicken your pace as you continue to move forward."

After failing that test, I needed a radical change. I needed to change my attitude in the face of failure. A change of attitude must start by transforming the way you think, which is later expressed in words and actions. "No more tears. It is time to change the very foundation, the deepest depths of my heart. I have lost a battle, but not the war."

9

"You can never cross the ocean until you have the courage
to lose sight of the shore."
Christopher Columbus

MAKE A RADICAL CHANGE

Read the list you wrote in activity number 6, at the end of Chapter 6, and aim to take that list to the next level. Make a plan regarding how you can not only improve, but become a true expert. Ask questions, do research, interview people who have achieved what you want to achieve. Make a radical change.

_____

_____

_____

_____

_____

_____

_____

_____

_____

_____

_____

_____

CHAPTER 10

∞

SIMPLIFY. SEEING PROBLEMS FROM A DIFFERENT PERSPECTIVE

"Let your net down on the right side of your boat, and you will catch some fish."

Jesus

Over the years, I have heard a story with some minor variations. I don't know if it's a true story, or the product of someone's imagination. Either way, I'd like to share it with you. Supposedly, it happened in front of a psychiatric hospital. The story says that an engineer was traveling from one city to another when suddenly his car hit a pothole in the road and he got a flat tire. The driver got out of the car and realized that not only had his tire gone flat, but the four nuts that kept it in place had popped off on impact. He was in big trouble now, because his car had a spare tire for emergencies, but no extra nuts.

A psychiatric patient who was watching the situation from the other side of the fence yelled to engineer:

— Hey, I have the solution to your problem!

The patient insisted, saying that he could help. So, since the engineer didn't want to listen to what he was sure would be an absurd suggestion, he replied:

— Buddy. I'm an engineer with a degree from a state university. Thanks, but we'll talk later.

A few minutes went by and the engineer had yet to solve his problem. The insane young man cried out again from the other side of the fence: Hey, I have the solution to your problem!

The engineer, feeling angry and desperate, replied:

— And what is the solution to my problem?

The young man replied quickly:

— Your car has four wheels, and each wheel has four nuts. Remove one nut from each wheel and you'll have three extra nuts. That way, each wheel will have three nuts. You can buy the missing nuts later.

Astonished by the young man's mathematical ability to add up the twelve nuts and then divide them by four, the engineer asked: How can it be that an insane person with such a talent for math is locked up in this hospital? —to which young man replied:

— Buddy, I'm in this hospital because I'm crazy, not stupid!

In mathematics, there is a technique called simplification that is used to solve problems. For example, it is much easier to go to a pizzeria and order half a pizza than to order 4/8 of a pizza, or 2/4 of a pizza.

"If your problem has a solution, why worry about it?
And if your problem doesn't have a solution, why worry about it?"
Chinese proverb

The most distant memory I have of the word *problem* goes back to elementary school. I remember the teacher would make us separate our problems into three categories or steps: assessment, operation and answer.

STEPS TO SOLVE PROBLEMS

Assessment: In the first step, you should assess the situation, or situations.

Operation: In the second step, you must choose which mathematical operation or formula you should use to find the solution to your problem.

Answer: The answer will be the result of the previous decisions; it could be correct or incorrect.

From a young age, I learned that the time it took me to figure out the answer to a problem varied depending on how I carried out the initial assessment. In other words, depending on the way I looked at the problem, the answer could be quite obvious or quite complicated. You must keep an open mind and be willing to try out different methods if you want to achieve your goals.

In the mathematics of success, you have to learn how to simplify. In your personal journey toward infinity, you will need to analyze problems from all angles. You must keep an open mind and be willing to try out different methods if you want to achieve your goals. In every situation that you encounter, make a habit of asking yourself if there might be another way of solving the dilemma. If so, is it the best option? Looking at problems from another point of view is vital if you want to reach infinity.

"You must keep an open mind and be willing to try out different methods if you want to achieve your goals."

After many hours of studying, my grade on that first test was not the one I had expected. I had failed my first test. How could that have happened? What had gone wrong? What was I doing wrong?

Some parents might ask themselves the same question when they find out that their teenage daughters are pregnant, or if when they find an illegal substance in their son's pockets. What went wrong? This is a very important question, but it is not the most appropriate one when considering a difficult situation, because it will make you focus on the mistakes and the negative elements of the event. The key question would be: What can I do to get the results I want? What can I do to help my daughter? What should I do so that my son can overcome his addiction?

The way in which we assess problems may lead us to think about certain solutions. In my experience, one of my classmates suggested another study method. He convinced me that he had gotten good results by doing "practice" tests. At first, I was against the idea, but those new practice tests turned out to be the solution to achieve my goal (passing my exams) so that I could get certified. After a month of using that method, I had passed three of the fourteen required tests and got my first certification. What changed? The second study method assessed the problem in a different way.

Dear reader, I want to tell you that if there is a problem in your life that you need to simplify, you can go back to step number one and reassess the situation from another perspective. I assure you that you will get better results.

AN ANECDOTE ABOUT SIMPLIFYING

When NASA starting sending astronauts into space, they discovered that pens would not work without gravity (or with zero gravity), because the ink would not flow on to the paper.

POSSIBLE SOLUTION NO. 1:

It took NASA six years and twelve million dollars to solve this problem. They developed a pen that worked under zero gravity, upside down, underwater, and which wrote on virtually any surface, including glass and in extreme temperatures.

POSSIBLE SOLUTION NO. 2:

On the other hand, what did the Russians do? They used a pencil!

10

"When everything seems to be going against you,
remember that the airplane takes off against the wind, not with it."
Henry Ford

ANOTHER PERSPECTIVE

For every challenge that separates you from your goal, write down at least 5 possible solutions. Analyze each and every one of them. Organize the possible solutions and try to implement them one at a time. Don't give up. Persevere until you are able to do it.

_____

_____

_____

_____

_____

_____

_____

_____

_____

_____

_____

_____

CHAPTER 11

∞

RESULTS. MY EXPERIENCE

"Wisdom is the daughter of experience."
Leonardo Da Vinci

L eonardo Da Vinci was one of the greatest geniuses of all time; he had a brilliant mind. He once said, "wisdom is the daughter of experience." So, in the following pages, I'd like to share my experience with the sole objective of encouraging you to achieve your goals, no matter what they are, even reaching infinity.

"One thorn of experience is worth a whole wilderness of warning."
James Russell Lowell

Up until now, we have shared a journey which started at zero. We have learned how important it is to stay positive, moving steadily toward infinity as we remove life's obstacles from our path. I have emphasized that we must identify clear and defined goals and develop a plan to achieve these goals. I have shared my experiences and results from the day I arrived in the United States up until the moment my dreams became a reality. I think of it as my version of the "American dream."

On August 4, years ago, I looked out the airplane window and saw the international airport of New York City. The plane was set to land in a little under an hour. That's when the flight attendants handed us immigration forms where we had to write down the address where each one of us would be staying. I asked myself: "Where am I going to live? Moreover, where am I going to sleep tonight?" That's the way life goes when you are young and your heart is full of hope. I started off on my trip to the United States without knowing where I was going, without close family members, without parents, siblings, cousins; in short, I didn't have anyone who shared my bloodline or my last name. "God, I need to make a deal with you. If you guide me through every step of my path, I will serve you for the rest of my life."

I had no idea how big the divine provision can be. It's true that I didn't have family in the United States, but I did have friends. The Duartes had been neighbors and friends of my family for years before immigrating to the United States. Their children were my childhood friends. The esteem and affection with which that family treated me was all the support I needed to make my way to a new country. There was just one detail: that family was in the process of moving to a new apartment.

God heard my prayer. That same day I arrived in the United States—not a day before nor a day after, and surely a result of divine providence—the Duarte family received the keys to their new apartment. That was my answer: not only did I spend that night sharing anecdotes and life lessons with their children, that family gave me shelter, love, and support for the next eleven months.

Mario, one of the children, recommended me at the restaurant where he worked, and for the next few months, it looked like things were going well for me. However, my dream was to study systems engineering and to graduate with a degree so that I could take advantage of my academic training. Meanwhile, tips were a great incentive to keep me working at the restaurant. Unfortunately, I was fired from that job before the end of the third month. Mario recommended me at another restaurant where they fired me on the first night. Thanks to the love and generosity that Mrs. Teresa Duarte and her family shared with me, I wasn't in need of any material thing, nor did I lack a roof over my head, but being unemployed in the United States was a big challenge for me.

A family that goes beyond your blood family is a spiritual family. I had accepted God's calling when I was 14 years old and decided to join God's family. I remember the words my pastor said to me at my baptism: "This certificate makes you a member of God's *global* family. Welcome to God's family." The Valerios were also a part of that family: Francisco, Dignora, Silvia, Helaine and Argenis. As a spiritual family, they gave me all the support I needed to stay faithful and go to church every weekend. Dignora introduced me to Pastor José Carpio, who, beyond giving me spiritual support, identified with me, became my mentor, and was practically a father to me.

Pastor Carpio was the one who offered me a job cleaning the temple at the church where he also ran a youth ministry. God, in His love, was undoubtedly guiding me through life. Around that time, I decided to enroll in English classes offered at a local college, but the high cost kept me from pursuing a career in engineering. I had to postpone my dream of studying until my situation became more favorable.

It was time to leave the nest of love and protection that I found at the Duarte and Valerio homes, because it was time for me to take off on my own flight. I thanked them for their unending support and found a room to rent. I barely had enough money to pay the rent, and I had to seek employment as a supermarket cashier in order to survive. For many weeks, I ate half of a roasted chicken for lunch, and the other half for dinner. Some ladies from the church occasionally offered me a plate of hot food, and I remember greatly appreciating their generosity. On the other hand, the winter weather was wreaking havoc on my Caribbean body as I adapted physically and emotionally to my new life.

I also met a brother at church whom I admired and respected because of how he selflessly served me. I will never forget the day he handed me a school bus driver's manual; he drove a school bus, and intended to give me free lessons so that I could learn to drive one as well. Henry has been more than a coach to me; he has been a friend and a father. Later on, life would give me the privilege of becoming his son-in-law. As part of the Cordero-Ledesma family, I felt an acceptance and love that we can only feel when God is guiding our steps.

God had prepared for me for the biggest surprise of my life. It happened on a Friday while I was preparing the youth ministry program. My eyes lit up when a young woman with long, black hair, elegantly dressed in winter clothing, walked through the church doors. I had never seen her before, and my heart jumped with joy as soon as I set eyes on her.

God gave me the opportunity to form a beautiful friendship with her, and from there we started dating, and finally, that beautiful woman became my wife; my queen, Brenda.

Upon meeting Brenda, I can definitely say that my journey toward infinity took a positive turn. With my new travel companion, I could see my goals more clearly, and my desire to accomplish them multiplied. We had to work hard to turn my goals and her goals into *our goals*, something that logically included making a home. Over time, the fruit of our love doubled, since three years after our wedding, we welcomed our twin sons, Christian and Christopher, into the world.

I went from working at the supermarket, to driving a school bus, to working at a money transfer agency and then working at a bookstore. Each of those jobs helped me to go a bit further in my journey. After almost a year of hard work, I got all my certifications. I was able to start working in my field as a contractor for the municipality of the City of New York, and then got a full-time job at the Administration for Children's Services (NYC ACS) in that same city. I did one more year of college and graduated with highest honors: *Summa Cum Laude.*

My work experience included working as a network engineer for the City of New York and the City of Yonkers. But I felt the most satisfaction when, on February 19, two days after having turned 33 years old, I returned to the classroom, and instead of taking my seat as a student, I went to the front of the class, ready to accept my position as an adjunct professor and teach a group of students. At last! I had reached my goal!

I hope that my experience inspires you! And that you are able to understand that you must persevere once you have made any decision, especially when faced with adverse circumstances. Remember that you must wrap yourself up in a positive faith, learn to accept the help of others, and stay true to your values and principles without cutting corners on the effort and sacrifices that will maximize your potential. Only then will you be able to make your dreams a reality. I can testify to that!

11

"Fall down seven times, get up eight."

Japanese proverb

EVALUATE YOUR RESULTS

Go back to activity number 10, at the end of Chapter 10, and evaluate your results. You should evaluate any result that has not been satisfactorily completed. If necessary, make a new list of 5 possible solutions that you had not tried before.

_____

_____

_____

_____

_____

_____

_____

_____

_____

_____

_____

_____

CHAPTER 12

∞

INFINITY. THE ALPHA AND THE OMEGA

"Mathematics is the alphabet in which God
has written the universe."
Galileo Galilei

The Creator is the source of all wisdom and science. His immeasurable love makes our existence possible. Dawn, rain, wind, sparrows, flowers, and the air we breathe are a testament to Him being the source of all life.

You must recognize that God is infinite, whether you know Him as Yahweh, Allah, the Supreme Mind, the Almighty, the God of the Heavens, or Jesus. If you are one of those who deny His existence because you don't understand Him, remember that if you, as a finite mortal, were to understand all things infinite and eternal, God would cease to be God. Today I invite you to open your heart to your Creator and accept that God is love.

"If it were possible for created beings to attain
a full understanding of God and His works, then, having reached
this point, there would be for them no further discovery of truth,

no growth in knowledge, no further development of mind or heart.
God would no longer be supreme; and man, having reached
the limit of knowledge and attainment, would cease to advance.
Let us thank God that it is not so. God is infinite."
White, E.G., "Steps to Christ" - page 109

FROM ZERO TO INFINITY represents my life's journey. Any person's insatiable search for earthly goals and objectives should culminate with an encounter that leads him to eternity: the largest goal that we can ever hope to achieve, our encounter with Jesus. In this world, every step you take will somehow change something in your life, or in the lives of others. Always avoid moving away from the main objective for which you came into this world.

All goals, as noble and important they may seem, lack true value if we do not make them part of a broader perspective that starts with infinity; that is, a divine perspective. All of your plans must begin and end with God.

"I am Alpha and Omega, the beginning and the end."
Jesus

And if you are reading this book at a young age, I would say: "Get up and go forth to conquer the world." If you are older, I would say: it is never too late to start. Fight for your ideals and make your life an inspiration to those around you. Learn from your mistakes, forgive yourself and keep moving forward. Never quit! Leave zero behind today. Put all your plans in God's hands and He will help you to achieve victory!

"I can do all things through Christ who strengthens me."

Your name_____

Allow me to use the following lines to thank you for your company on this journey that started at zero, and whose final destination is infinity. Throughout our journey, we have seen that life abides by principles similar to those found in mathematics. I call this the mathematics of success. I hope you have enjoyed reading this book, and it is my greatest wish that our paths cross in eternity, where we will be able enjoy the undeserved privilege of having reached the final goal: *The Eternal Kingdom of God's infinite love.*

AUTHOR BIOGRAPHY

Despite his humble beginnings, Edwin De Paula has reached his dreams and professional goals.

Edwin has worked as network engineer for the City of New York and the City of Yonkers, as well as for private institutions. He has also worked as an adjunct professor of network communications.

He has shared his life with his wife, Brenda, for almost a decade. God has blessed their union with twin sons: Christian and Christopher.

Today, as well as writing and offering seminars and lectures, the author is a Master's degree candidate at Andrews University in Berrien Springs, Michigan.

To get in touch with the author
or to order additional copies of

FROM

ZERO

TO

INFINITY

A practical and effective guide to reach your goals
using the mathematics of success
by Edwin De Paula
ISBN-10: 0692327878* ISBN-13: 978-0692327876
Visit our pages for **Zero to Infinity**:
Web: www.zerotoinfinity.org
Facebook: @depaulaministries
Twitter: @zerotoinfinity_
Instagram: @zerotoinfinity_

You may also scan the QR code on your smart phone
to enter our web site.

This book is also available in its Spanish title:
Del Cero al Infinito

at www.amazon.com